DEDICATION

This book is dediated to my daughter Sheila, and grand-daughters
Tiffany and Tiara.

ACKNOWLEDGEMENT

I would like to thank all that took the time to travel with me along my journey. S. and D. Associates, my people forever, and Evette Bliey for your creative input.

Special thanks to Corrinne, Glenda McGee, Elaine Redway, Mike Chong, Suzette Bliey, Coach Anita at WW, Fresno, and Ms. Angela White from Silver Lining Entertainment, LLC.

To the young ones beginning their journey Joi Carter, Anjale' Oberton, Amanda Thompson, Honey D., Kayla L., and Katie Thompson. This is for all of you to stay focused.

Thank you to the art department Nathanael Larsen, Marlon Brooks, and Madeline La Rose.

DISCLAIMER

Any resemblance to any actual persons, scenarios, or events and companies is purely
coincidental.

TABLE OF CONTENTS

Where are you in these poems?

If you read between the lines

Do you think you'll find someone

Who resembles you?

YOUR THOUGHTS

Me Myself and I and Maybe You

YOUR THOUGHTS

THE HEART IS THE DIARY OF THE SOUL

It's been written that words are the voice of the heart
And if I am to believe these words to be true
Is it not fair to assume
The heart to be the diary of the soul

For into it I cast my pain, pleasure, love, and hate
My securities and insecurities
Disappointments and accomplishments as well
I lock them all away in my heart each day
With the hope for a better tomorrow

Yes, it is with the same heart
That renders me sensual one moment
And deems me senseless the next
That I reach into my soul and share it all
And lock it away for another day

Oh, heart of mine with each beat, you remind me
Of the life with which I've been blessed
And although you know of all my errors
You allow me no regrets

For the key to my life is in your lock
And the pages are waiting to be turned
Oh, Dear Diary of the Heart
You are the true reflection of my soul, allowing me
To put it all into words

By S.A. Thompson

Me Myself and I and Maybe You

YOUR THOUGHTS

YOUR THOUGHTS

Ladies, let's confess it, address it, and move on.

By S.A. Thompson

YOUR THOUGHTS

Me Myself and I and Maybe You

YOUR THOUGHTS

THE MIRROR IN MY EYE

I looked in the mirror today and saw the woman

Who had once walked away

Leaving hopes and dreams behind

Never once thinking they would be realized

Succumbing to a life of negativity

Until I decided to set myself free

I determined my worth not by what others thought

Nor by the things little girls are taught

Just smile, be pretty, stay skinny, and learn to cook

That never appealed to me. I preferred to read a book

The mirror in my eye showed the new true reflection

Of the woman I'm becoming through sheer determination

The woman I am meant to be… to be continued

By S.A. Thompson

Me Myself and I and Maybe You

YOUR THOUGHTS

Me Myself and I and Maybe You

YOUR THOUGHTS

ARE YOU LISTENING

When you have a lot to say about life and no one listens

You may want to write

When you have a lot to say about life and no one listens

You may want to fight

When you have a lot to say about life and no one listens

You may want to cry

When you have a lot to say about life and no one listens

You may want to die

But, no, not me, I wouldn't give you the satisfaction

And there will be no more begging you to lend me your ear

I know you don't want to hear the truth; I can see it in your eyes

Yet, now you're faint out of fear after looking into mine

I can use my words to destroy you and it would be well deserved

Or I can choose to forgive you according to The Word

It's my choice, so now let me ask you

Are you listening

By S.A. Thompson

YOUR THOUGHTS

Me Myself and I and Maybe You

YOUR THOUGHTS

ARE YOU SURE

Are you praying for one thing

While hoping for another

Your kingdom come

Your will be done

Is what you say when you pray

But can we see it's what you want

By the way, you live your life each day

Don't be fooled by the trappings

And begin confusing right from wrong

Allowing for temporary pleasures

That you know in your heart are wrong

Are you praying for one thing

While hoping for another

Are you sure about what it is you want

By S.A. Thompson

Me Myself and I and Maybe You

YOUR THOUGHTS

YOUR THOUGHTS

Me Myself and I and Maybe You

Boundaries and bridges

Think hard and long before

You set up your boundaries

And before you burn those bridges

The end results may surprise you.

YOUR THOUGHTS

Me Myself and I and Maybe You

YOUR THOUGHTS

THE WALL

I built a wall around me for protection

It is to head off all obvious deception

You see I can tell by your eyes

That your heart is full of lies

And your words are apart

Of a conspiracy to devalue me

By keeping my mind distracted

Because of the potential, you see in me

Viewing it as a threat to your masculinity

Yes, I have seen that look before

You are not the first to come through

The door and like you

There was no love in their eyes

And still, I refuse to compromise

The Wall is my protection

By S.A. Thompson

Me Myself and I and Maybe You

YOUR THOUGHTS

YOUR THOUGHTS

DID YOU FORGET

Sometimes we look for reasons to be able to justify the pain we cause each other

Somehow, we forget the reasons we once loved each other

We forget reaching out to each other during our trials and loses

We forget holding each other as we cried

We forget the smiles of joy we put on each other's faces when we shared good news

We forget holding each other so tight neither of us could breathe

Holding hands and looking into the eyes of each other so tenderly

Our favorite song and the cute nicknames we gave each other

Now when you speak your words are harsh and bitter as if I'm a stranger

Your eyes that once looked at me lovingly now look through me as if I don't exist

And so now my question to you is

Did you forget

By S.A. Thompson

YOUR THOUGHTS

YOUR THOUGHTS

DON'T HIDE

You hide in the dark behind a screen mocking me and others

Making sure you can't be seen

You and your insecurities, hurt, and pain

You've never felt good enough always weighed down by shame

Yes, you strike out at me because I have chosen

To let others see I value myself and what I think

Of the woman, I have become

All the time you're wishing that woman was you

Yes, you are longing to be the person being seen

Not having to hide in the dark behind a screen

Striking out at me and others for choosing to live our lives

While you are hiding in the dark allowing yourself to be deprived

Of a life worth stepping away from behind the screen.

Don't hide.

By S.A. Thompson

Me Myself and I and Maybe You

YOUR THOUGHTS

Me Myself and I and Maybe You

YOUR THOUGHTS

DON'T FORGET WHO YOU ARE

He may be the man of your dreams

But in reality, what does that mean

It means he will be your provider and protector

Your confidant and best friend

But what happens in between

Does it mean you give up on your dreams

No, it means he should be your biggest cheerleader

And source of motivation

Helping you accomplish all the things that make you

Who you are

By S.A. Thompson

YOUR THOUGHTS

Me Myself and I and Maybe You

YOUR THOUGHTS

I AM HAPPY

I am happy with who I was yesterday

I am happy with who I am today

I am happy with who I will be tomorrow

I am not one for conformity

Knowing there will never be another me

Therein lies my authenticity

So yes, I am happy

And you can't take that away from me.

By S.A. Thompson

Me Myself and I and Maybe You

YOUR THOUGHTS

Me Myself and I and Maybe You

YOUR THOUGHTS

DISTRACTION

You have become a distraction

I knew it was too good to be true

So, I'm not going to be able to

Take this journey with you

You have become a distraction

And that is not good

Because I'm not handling my business

The way I know I should

I have stopped focusing on my own goals

And making my dreams come true

No longer a priority while distracted by you

My hopes of a bright future are going up in smoke

You are holding me back not lifting me up

And the sad thing is you call it love

Your lack of goals and direction has become a concern

You have ignored opportunities and want me to do the same

Yes, you have become a distraction

And that no longer works for me

I can no longer sacrifice my dreams

It is time to set myself free

By S.A. Thompson

Me Myself and I and Maybe You

YOUR THOUGHTS

YOUR THOUGHTS

You'll get through it
It's all good, just stay strong
You're making good choices
We are all proud of you.

Me Myself and I and Maybe You

YOUR THOUGHTS

Me Myself and I and Maybe You

YOUR THOUGHTS

FINDING MY WAY

Round and round I go

When I am going to stop

I don't know

Where I am going to stop

I don't know

Who I will be when I stop

I don't know

There have been so many ups and downs

Twist and turns and broken promises along the way

So right now, it's impossible for me to say

But I will never give up hoping that tomorrow

Maybe a better day for me to find my way

By S.A. Thompson

Me Myself and I and Maybe You

YOUR THOUGHTS

Me Myself and I and Maybe You

YOUR THOUGHTS

THE ANSWER

So many have suffered in silence

So many have struggled with shame

So many continue wondering

If they were to blame

So many are searching for the answer

To the question "Why Me?"

Please help them find the answer

As it is the key to their dignity

By S.A. Thompson

YOUR THOUGHTS

YOUR THOUGHTS

I HAVE BEEN THINKING ABOUT YOU

I have been thinking about you

Yes, it was so long ago

But I wanted to reach out

To you just to let you know

Time has been good to me

Helping to heal old wounds

How about you

I hope life has been good to you too

Do you ever think about me

Or do you still feel I was to blame

We were both so young

And acted foolishly saying and

Doing things to set ourselves free

Yes, I have been thinking about you

Because the years are passing swiftly

And there is not much time to say,

Despite the way things ended

You are still in my heart today

I have been thinking about you

By S.A. Thompson

YOUR THOUGHTS

Me Myself and I and Maybe You

YOUR THOUGHTS

I WONDER

Most people believe they are going to Heaven

When they die, and I often wonder why

If people can't get along here on Earth

Then how do they qualify

To live in a place where God is not partial

And his actions have proved he values all of our lives

Yes, prejudice is something he won't tolerate

There is no room for hatred where he resides

Besides, he has given us this place

For the righteous to reside forever

And regarding that place, there is no compromise

So, I wonder

By S.A. Thompson

Me Myself and I and Maybe You

YOUR THOUGHTS

Me Myself and I and Maybe You

YOUR THOUGHTS

KEEPING UP APPEARANCES

So, you're keeping up appearances

But for whose sake

I can tell by the look in your eyes

You are ready to break

It's time to make a decision

Be truthful with yourself

Remember this is about you nobody else

Yes, listen to your inner voice

Is this really what you had in mind

When you made your choice

Because it's not too late to rectify

Your obvious mistake

Stop keeping up appearances

For really others sake

Forget about what people may say

Remember, it is your life

At the end of the day.

By S.A. Thompson

YOUR THOUGHTS

YOUR THOUGHTS

JOURNEY THROUGH MY VISION

I never knew who I was

Why I was

Or where I was, until today

I had visions of getting myself out of this darkness

I've trapped myself in called a "Life"

I've searched myself for the missing pieces of my soul

So that I would be able to see myself complete

No longer in darkness, but in the "Light of Life"

A real life full of love, emotion, passion, and truth

A truth about me, and who I am

That will set me free today and forever

No, my vision is not of the way you look at me

Or the way you feel

Nor the smell of you so close to me

But I saw for the first time

The very first time

Who I was

Why I am, who I am and

Where I will be tomorrow

If I love myself, as much as I do

You and you and you!

There isn't anything I can't do

So, you see, I've finally come to realize

It's really about how I see myself

Through my own eyes

And if I will allow you

To accompany me through my journey

By S.A. Thompson

Me Myself and I and Maybe You

YOUR THOUGHTS

Me Myself and I and Maybe You

YOUR THOUGHTS

Demand no less than the best from yourself

Don't wait on someone else to start the engine

Of your life.

Me Myself and I and Maybe You

YOUR THOUGHTS

YOUR THOUGHTS

YOUR WORTH

It is sad when you feel

You have nothing to offer

And bring nothing to the table

Only to find that to him

You are as divine as an exquisite

Seven-course gourmet meal

And to him the fine wine and china

Mean nothing at all if he is dining alone

Without the sound of your voice

Tickling his ears between each course

So, take your place, know your worth,

You are worthy, of so much more.

By S.A. Thompson

Me Myself and I and Maybe You

YOUR THOUGHTS

Me Myself and I and Maybe You

YOUR THOUGHTS

PLANS

Your best-made plans will be dismantled

And sadly, put on hold

If you attach yourself to someone

Who clearly has no direction or goals

Distance yourself before it's too late

And pick up where you left off

You're destined for great things

It's time to let go and move on

By S.A. Thompson

YOUR THOUGHTS

Me Myself and I and Maybe You

YOUR THOUGHTS

NOT BROKEN

He held me in his arms and whispered in my ear

"I can fix you"

I looked him in the eyes, smiled, and said

"Fix me, honey I'm not broken"

By S.A. Thompson

Me Myself and I and Maybe You

YOUR THOUGHTS

Me Myself and I and Maybe You

YOUR THOUGHTS

REWIRED

Do you remember who you are

Your likes, dislikes, hobbies, hopes and dreams

I would think that what attracted a person to you

Is what they would want you to continue to be

And you the same for the other, in addition to

Growing together in perfect harmony

So far it sounds like a winner, but sometimes there's

A catch, you hit a bump in the road and you find yourself

Being rewired to accommodate someone else's vision of you

If it works for you fine, if not look that someone in the eye

So, they recognize who the person is they were attracted to

and there's no need to rewire you.

By S.A. Thompson

Me Myself and I and Maybe You

YOUR THOUGHTS

Me Myself and I and Maybe You

YOUR THOUGHTS

NOT PARTIAL

If you can't live in peace on earth

Why do you think heaven will be better

God is not partial he's made that clear

By creating a variety of colors of skin

Eyes and hair

What part of the message to love your brother

Did you not hear

And why do you find it

So hard to adhere

No, he's not partial

By now it should be clear

Because when it was written that one day

The righteous will inherit the Earth

It will include all of us in a variety of colors

Because God is not partial

He made no mistakes.

By S.A. Thompson

Me Myself and I and Maybe You

YOUR THOUGHTS

Me Myself and I and Maybe You

YOUR THOUGHTS

SECRETS

You say you have a story to tell

And you don't know where to start

You say once you start talking

It will break a lot of hearts

It was Oprah, Dr's Oz, and Phil

After watching them you know the drill

The truth is the light they say

It supposed to set you free

But the fact is when you tell the truth

You become the enemy

The secrets that have been swept away

Under the rugs and in the closets

Begin to make some uncomfortable

With the thought of their dislodging

Those who chose to look the other way

And those who promised they would never say

They are stuttering and stammering looking for an excuse

To justify their allowing not preventing the abuse

You say you have a story to tell and it won't be pretty

And now that you have found the strength

What you don't need is our pity

By S.A. Thompson

YOUR THOUGHTS

Me Myself and I and Maybe You

YOUR THOUGHTS

.

THE HYPE

If you are waiting on that knight in shining armor

Don't believe the hype

Besides, if he showed up on his white horse

He probably wouldn't be your type

By S.A. Thompson

Me Myself and I and Maybe You

YOUR THOUGHTS

YOUR THOUGHTS

You've taken a self-reflective journey

And what did you learn?

Any and every obstacle can be overturned

Stay focused

Me Myself and I and Maybe You

YOUR THOUGHTS

YOUR THOUGHTS

TREASURE ME

Treasure me or take possession of me

Which do you think I prefer

When you first looked into my eyes

Did you view me as a prize

Or just another piece of property

You wanted to possess

You who love being known

For only acquiring the best

You pursued me with vigor

Which led me to believe

That if I allowed myself

To be swept off my feet

You would treat me like a queen

Instead, I sit alone, in this gilded cage

You refer to as our home on full display

For all to see how well you're providing for me

I was so wrong and sadly my dreams

Of you treasuring me are far and few between

Know that as often as you feel the need to show

That I am your possession

I would still prefer you treasure, yes

Treasure Me

By S.A. Thompson

Me Myself and I and Maybe You

YOUR THOUGHTS

YOUR THOUGHTS

YESTERDAY, TODAY, AND TOMORROW

Which will bring the most sorrow

Yesterday is gone but I still have the wounds

Of a life lived way to soon

Today, I know what adjustments need to be made

Before I can truly say I learned the hard way

Tomorrow may be too late to make amends

As COVID is taking so many family members and friends

Hopefully, I can still pay homage to what may have been

If we had found forgiveness before the end

By S.A. Thompson

YOUR THOUGHTS

Me Myself and I and Maybe You

YOUR THOUGHTS

WHEN HE ASKS ABOUT YOU

When he asks about you

What should I say

When we stopped loving one another

You just walked away

It was hard on us both your son and me

Yet, I need you to know I did try

I did all I could, just like a mother should

Now here I stand ready to lay our son to rest

And you're nowhere to be found

As they lower him into the ground

I wish you had reached out from time to time

It may have prevented his life's decline

Yes, it was you he longed for and that's why

We are here today

He needed you to show him there was another way

To be a real man

Now he will never again ask about you

By S.A. Thompson

YOUR THOUGHTS

YOUR THOUGHTS

Me Myself and I and Maybe You

ME

YOUR THOUGHTS

Me Myself and I and Maybe You

YOUR THOUGHTS

AUTHOR'S PAGE

S. A. Thompson, a native of New York, is an author, (What's Done In The Dark) and poet. Her latest work "Me Myself and I and Maybe You", a poetry book/journal, offers the authors perspective on several ongoing women's issues.

"Distraction", appaulds women who are staying focused on their purpose and journey. "Did You Forget?" is a reminder of when things were good between you and yours. "Don't Hide" is a clap back at cyberbullies. "When He Asks About You" is an ode to the single parent, a real tearjerker. And "The Answer" is a sobering reality check.

S. A. Thompson currently resides in California. When she is not writing she is baking up a storm, reading, and looking forward to traveling again and spending time with her family and meeting the new additions to the family.

Made in the USA
Columbia, SC
16 August 2021

42991806R00057